# Meet t[illegible]ple



# The Cheasies

First Published in Great Britain in 2008
by NightHawk Publishing



All characters and places in this publication are fictitious and any resemblance to any places or real persons, both living and dead is purely coincidental. Character names are fictitious and not associated in any way to any type of real cheese, cheese production process, cheese area, cheese trademark or cheese association.

A CIP catalogue record for this book is available from the British Library

ISBN 978-0-9559788-1-4

**www.cheesepeople.co.uk**

Visit our website for more books, stories and Cheese People information

An audio version of our books is also available

# The Cheese People

## Introduction

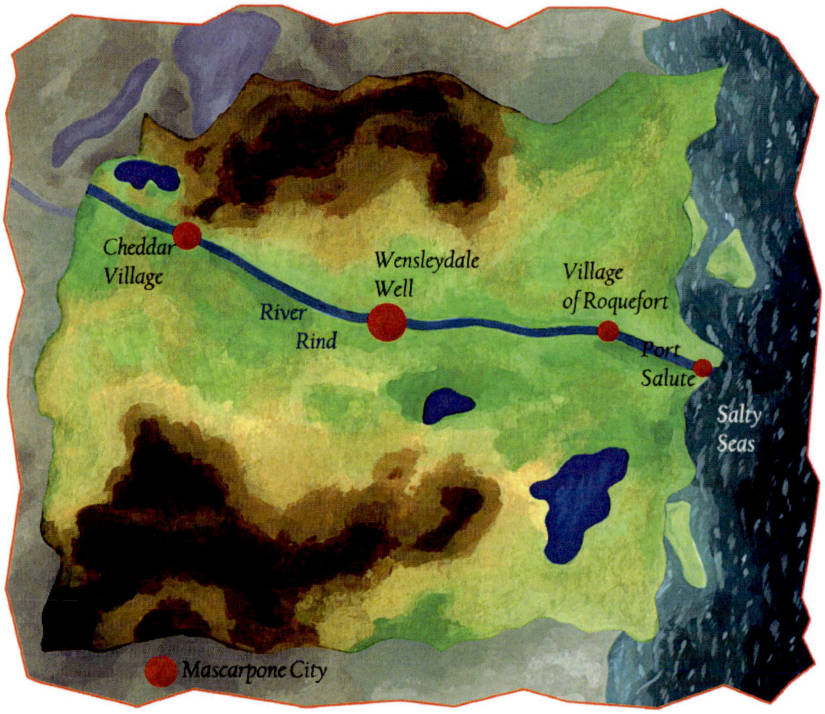


Hello, we're The Cheese People
and we live in Wensleydale Vale.
This book will introduce you to us
and we hope you enjoy the tale.

You'll meet Mozzarella Mike,
unless he's on his bike,
and also the Count of Boursin.
I'm sure Parmesan Pete,
will have time to meet,
especially if you're a fan.

You'll meet Stilton Peters, Lucy Leicester, and we may track down Monteray Jack.
Lincolnshire Lynne, may well pop in, unless she's training on the track.

You'll meet Bobby Blue, Sergeant String and may even meet Gary the Goat.
But he's often away, well that's what they say, so he may not be on his boat.

You'll meet Caerphilly Kate, she won't be late, and also the beautiful Bri-Anne.
We'll knock on the door, of the Duke of Roquefort, now he's an interesting man.

So on to the tale, of those living in the Vale, an interesting bunch of folk.
From young to old, from shy to bold, and a few like a good laugh and joke.

## Charlie Cheshire

Charlie Cheshire is a very wise man, and works for the Wensleydale Gazette.
He knows what's happening all the time, and everyone in the Vale he has met.

His job is to discover what's going on in the Vale,
and to write useful, and interesting news.
He enjoys his job, investigating and reporting,
and discovering people's opinions and views.

He's good at his job, he's fantastic with people,
and is married with a beautiful daughter.
He worked very hard, to get to where he is,
and is very proud of being a reporter.

## Arianna Bella

Arianna Bella used to work in a wine cellar, and now looks after children from home.
She has two brothers, helps out local mothers, but really prefers being on her own.

She dislikes most adults, because they try to find faults,
and this is why she's quiet and shy.
She used to go out of her way, to speak to people every day,
but now she doesn't even try.

She loves her daughter to bits, apart from her little fits,
and makes sure she's well looked after.
She seems quiet and shy, and often you'll see her cry,
but at home she's full of joy and laughter.

# Baby Bella

She's the daughter of Arianna, colourful like a banana,
and is wise for a girl aged just six years.
She's intelligent, smart, speaks from her little heart,
and loves coming up with new ideas.

She can laugh for an hour, has lots of energy and power,
and her imagination is often out of control.
She has a lot of good friends, likes to play 'pretends',
and loves listening to Elvis and rock and roll.

She's the brightest pupil in her class, learns very fast,
and when she's old, she wants to be a vet.
She loves reading, writing, hates violence and fighting,
and her mouse 'Michael', is her favourite pet.

# Monterey Jack

An adventurer, fit and healthy, that's our
Monterey Jack.
By the time you're half way up the mountain,
he'd have been there twice and back.

He works in the activity centre, close to Cheddar caves.
He has a dog called 'Monty' and courage like Indian braves.

He loves spending his time climbing mountains and hills,
and is a bit of an adrenalin junkie.
You should see the way, he climbs up those rocks,
anyone would think he's a monkey.

# Freddie Feta

Freddie Feta wants his life to get better, but he's often unhappy and sad.
Things never go right, his life's a big fight, and this makes him very mad.

He's very, very precise, but kind and also nice,
and works as a self-employed electrician.
He's cool like snow, there's nothing he doesn't know,
he's just miserable and lacks any vision.

He lives on his own, he's unhappy and likes to moan,
and wishes he could stop his complaining.
And when he goes outdoors, he thinks he's the cause,
of the clouds and the reason for it raining.

# The Duke of Roquefort

The Duke of Roquefort, has never been abroad, and is a real character in the Vale.
He's honest, loyal, from a family that is Royal, and can tell you an interesting tale.

He has blue blood in his veins, his family own trains,
and he's a very traditional sort of man.
He prefers old to new, talks about 'what he used to do'
and goes out with beautiful Brie-Anne.

Now over the years, he's conquered a few fears,
and recently went up in a plane.
And as soon as it had landed, he quickly demanded,
that the Captain took off once again.

## Brie-Anne

Brie-Anne is an elegant and beautiful woman, living in the Village of Roquefort.
She has a personal income and lots of money, so there's nothing she can't afford.

She's a well spoken, stylish and pretty woman,
who is always very well dressed.
And if you're lucky enough to meet with her,
I think you'll be very impressed.

She likes having fun, meeting her friends,
and is always on the move.
And if you take her to meet your parents,
you know that they'd approve.

## The Count of Boursin

The Count of Boursin is a very wealthy man,
with both money and imagination.
He has twelve cars and a race track around his house,
a boat, two trains and a station.

He worships his children Adam and Eve,
and once bought them a railway train.
And not the type you play with in your bedroom,
this was real and the size of a plane!

He owns Boursin Private Banking, the largest bank in the Vale,
and works there three days every week.
He knows eight different languages, including German and French,
and now he's learning to speak Greek.

## Adam and Eve

Adam and Eve are beautiful twins,
living with their father the Count of Boursin.
One of them likes to think things through,
and the other thinks, 'Oh yes I can'.

Adam is sporty and physical,
Eve is quick and bright.

Adam will use his strength to win,
Eve will think it right.

## Emily Gouda

Emily Gouda has been a cook for the Count,
for just over twenty five years.
She's one of the greatest cooks in the world,
admired by all of her peers.

She can create a feast from a cupboard bare,
and will leave all her guests feeling full.
She once made a meal for eighty nine people,
using crab, white shark and a seagull.

She lives with the Count, and looks after the twins,
it's a job that she really enjoys.
She likes painting and drawing, has a habit of snoring,
you don't want to hear that noise!

# Swiss Chris

Swiss works in the Camembert Country Club, looking after the needs of each guest.
It's a very posh 'members only' club, and you'll never find anyone in a vest.

To join the club you need a smart range of clothes,
and over six thousand pounds a year.
There's currently a waiting list of forty five names,
and they only serve wine, never beer.

Swiss is totally amazing at organising and arranging,
and once planned a big party in Korea.
It took her forty two days just to plan the event,
and the party nearly lasted a year.

# Emma Emmental

One of the most mysterious women in the Vale, is Emma Emmental,
although she appears quite ordinary, so you would never tell.

She dresses in plain and simple clothes,
and has a kind of hippy look.
But underneath this everyday person,
there's wisdom not found in a book.

She likes helping others, is caring and kind,
and will do anything to help people out.
She has a comforting voice, relaxing and calm,
so I doubt you'll ever hear her shout.

## Ted Leicester

Ted Leicester is a powerful man, and dresses like someone aged thirty.
He's really forty nine, is obsessed with time and hates things untidy or dirty.

He has a difficult job running Wensleydale Council,
and works ten hours every day.
But on Friday at four, he shuts his office door,
and drives to the country to get away.

His daughter Lucy studies art at University,
and lives with him at his address.
He doesn't mind having her around,
it's just that she leaves such a mess!

## Lucy Leicester

Lucy Leicester is outgoing and fun,
with a personality that's outrageous.
She doesn't think, loves life, food and drink,
and that's why her body's curvaceous.

She studies art at University, when she remembers to turn up,
and is clumsy and makes a lot of mess.
She loves her boyfriend very much, likes to kiss and touch,
but causes him a great deal of stress.

She has a mind of her own, hates being alone,
and loves talking about things that aren't right.
She once started talking, at six in the morning,
and continued until nine o'clock that night.

## Stilton Peters

Stilton loves Lucy, loves physics even more,
and this is how he spends most of his time.
He studies and studies, reads all day long,
and has an IQ of two hundred and nine.

He's seen as being lazy, which is totally crazy,
he just prefers to read good books.
He loves being with Lucy, thinks she's attractive,
and not just because of her looks.

He dislikes taking risks, is very careful, and does things with a great deal of care.
He can be very slow and a little too careful, and Lucy wants him to restyle his hair!

## Parmesan Pete

Parmesan Pete is ever so sweet, and he's a very talented man.
He plays professional footballer for Wensleydale Wanderers,
and Rachel Ricotta is his number one fan.

He's a talented player, very fast and very fit,
and on the pitch he attacks and defends.
When not playing football, his favourite activity,
you'll find him behind a camera lens.

He owns a shop, specialising in sports photography,
it's a great job and one that he likes.
But if he could choose any job, any job in the world,
it would be something to do with bikes.

## Rachel Ricotta

Rachel Ricotta is great at her job, and can do anything with your hair.
Visit her salon, explain what you're thinking, she'll help then and there.

She has a great reputation, but if you want an appointment,
you're going to have to wait.
But this is worthwhile, because when she has finished,
you'll walk out looking just great!

She started her business at the age of seventeen,
and since then it's grown and grown.
There are now three people working in her salon,
but at the start she was all on her own.

## Sergeant String

Sergeant String believes in one thing,
things are either wrong or right.
He likes a simple life, without complication,
and believes things are black or white.

But this simple belief has caused much grief,
because most people think he's too tough.
He just deals with the facts, is not too relaxed,
and knows when enough, is enough.

He doesn't mess around, he gets straight to the point,
and some people don't like his ways.
But what he has found, is that by not messing around,
he get's results in hours, not days.

## Bobby Blue

Bobby Blue is the local policeman, and makes sure that people keep to the law.
He's the man you want to see around, but never want him to knock on your door.

He questions, questions, then questions again,
and always uncovers the truth.
He once spoke to a family for forty two hours,
just to locate a missing tooth.

He's very fair and likes to know the facts,
before deciding what action he'll take.
He listens to both sides, before he decides,
and never once has he made a mistake.

## Mozzarella Mike

Mozzarella Mike is the local mechanic,
with a passion for cars, trucks and bikes.
He has a very relaxed approach to life,
and thinks he can do what he likes.

He enjoys fixing engines, loves off road vehicles,
and likes driving over rocks, dirt and stones.
He drives around without a care in the world,
and one day he'll break all his bones.

He loves speed, noise and power, the wind in his hair,
and likes fixing and repairing old cars.
He loves music and dance, and if given a chance,
would build a rocket and go to the stars.

## Caerphilly Kate

Caerphilly Kate hates being late, and is always on time.
She's never late, hates to wait, but if early, she's just fine.

All her rooms have a clock, she likes the tick and tock,
and every day checks that they're right.
She double locks her doors, has no gaps in her floors,
and sleeps for seven hours every night.

She records where she's been, what she's done, who she's seen,
and has a special room where this is kept.

She eats her food at a certain time, has never committed a crime,
and knows exactly how long she has slept.

## Gary the Goat

Gary the Goat is a bit of a loner, and likes to keep out of the public eye.
You won't see him in the day, he likes it this way, nobody understands why.

He keeps himself to himself, along with his secret,
something he cannot explain.
If other people knew, they'd be in great danger,
he did this once, never again.

He lives on a boat, docked in Port Salute,
because there he attracts little attention.
People often say, what are you doing today,
he replies that he's going to a convention.

## Dorothy Double-Gloucester

Dorothy Double-Gloucester is a serious woman,
responsible for running her school.
With seven children of her own, school and home,
she has a very important golden rule.

She plans every day in an organised way, to make sure things get done.
She plans study, work and breaks, makes no mistakes, and then has fun.

She plans the timetable, to ensure students are able, to get to where they need to go.
She walks around, every part of the school ground, there's nothing she doesn't know.

## Edam Rees-Jones

Edam Rees-Jones has perfectly shaped bones, and skin smoother than fine china.
With beautiful lips, beauty to launch a thousand ships, she wants to be a designer.

She's caring and kind, looks after her body and mind,
and loves fashion design, animals and clothes.
She rushes here, rushes there, never a minute to spare,
where she finds the energy, no one knows.

She loves vegetables, fruit and fish,
tuna salad is her favourite dish,
and she exercises every day to stay healthy.

She's also building brick by brick,
an animal shelter for the sick,
because she'd prefer to help them, than be wealthy.

## Philadelphia Fred

Philadelphia Fred spends his mornings in bed and then at one,
he goes to work in the 'Cotswolds' café.
The job is easy, with no stress, just serving and clearing mess,
and he does this for the rest of the day.

He likes meeting people new, finding out what they do,
and enjoys chatting to the guests.
Now he's retired, he finds he gets tired,
and has to stop to take little rests.

Many people go in, just to meet him, normally after going to the lakes.
Talking to everyone and having fun, the owner doesn't mind these breaks.

## The Melted Cheese

Please understand this is no ordinary band, they are unique with a style of their own.
When new, there fans numbered forty two, but now their popularity has really grown.

Music is there passion, they may lack style and fashion,
but make up for this in the music they play.
There music is loud, they get thousands in the crowd,
and you'll be singing their songs all day.

They're close to becoming big, getting paid well to play a gig,
and may soon be able to make it a career.
They practice every single day, plan to be around to stay,
and want to play at Glastonbury next year.

## Christian Cracker

Christian Cracker is a keen back packer, and goes camping whenever he can.
He loves open space, the wind in his face, and is an outdoors sort of man.

He enjoys the simple life, spending time with his wife,
and really loves walking his dogs.
He has a beautiful house, he built all by himself,
all from *'forest friendly'* logs.

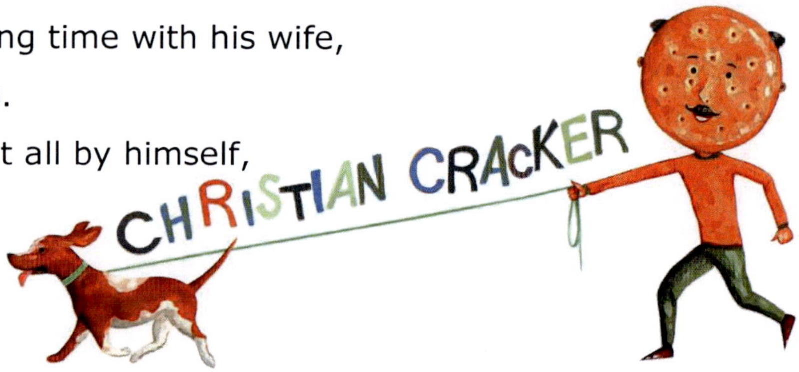


He spends lots of time indoors, studying different laws,
and has to read a lot of legal books.
But he's happier and feels free, working for this charity,
in his last job he had to help crooks.

## Patrick Pickle

Patrick Pickle is not very nice, and wears clothes that are dirty and faded.
He's nasty indeed, always disagrees, and cannot be easily persuaded.

He dislikes Cheeses, does as he pleases and is nasty to people in the Vale.
He hates success, likes causing stress and loves to see other people fail.

He's likes to scream and shout, causes upset when he's about,
and likes to get involved at the beginning.
But he gets bored half way through, when he's done all he can do,
and all he really cares about, is winning.

## Tom Geanté

Tom Geanté loves a glass of Chianti,
and enjoys the finer things in life.
Honey from bees, chunks of fresh cheese,
and evenings at home with his wife.

He has a flat in St Tropez, a house in Sydney Bay,
and a beautiful villa in Spain.
He has a castle in Milan, a plush palace in Pakistan,
and even owns his own plane.

He has an antique Porsche Carrera, a Jaguar that's even rarer,
and at weekends he drives an Aston Martin.
He owns three golf courses, has eighteen race horses,
and is making a film that he'll star in.

## Manchego Matt

Manchego Matt used to be fat, but recently lost a lot of weight.
Even sat, his stomach is flat and he can get through his garden gate.

He can now see his feet, sit comfortably on a seat,
and can slide very easily into a car.
He can tie his own shoes, use public loos,
and can also rest his arms on the bar.

He can cross any bridge, walk past his kitchen fridge,
and in doorways he no longer gets stuck.
He's ok being weighed, can skate and roller blade,
without needing to be pulled by a truck.

## Cotswold Camilla

Cotswold Camilla is as strong as a gorilla, and loves to train in the gym.
She trains every night, knows how to fight, and is incredibly fit and slim.

She knows what to do, one attacker or a few,
she is small and doesn't look strong.
But she has this sort of look, you see in a book,
about karate masters in Hong Kong.

Confident inside, she is happy to hide, the fact that she's a natural born fighter.
Not making a first move, with nothing to prove, walking quietly away is politer.

## Wensleydale Gayle

Wensleydale Gayle hates looking pale, and spends most of her time outdoors.
Walking in the hills, exploring old mills, she often walks for eight hours or more.

She's ninety five, can still walk and drive,
and keeps herself very, very busy.
She's young at heart, likes an early start,
and loves drinking white wine, cool and fizzy.

Her husband passed away, on the second of last May,
and it still feels strange being on her own.
She misses their conversation, meeting him at the station,
and talking to him on his mobile phone.

She misses their holidays in the Bahamas, his smelly old pyjamas,
and the times when he forgot to turn out the light.
She misses his special smell, looking after him when unwell,
but most of all she misses his kiss, last thing at night.

# Penny - Y - Fenni

Penny-Y-Fenni is careful with every penny, and doesn't like wasting it at all.
She lost her job last week, can't eat or sleep, and feels about six inches tall.

She's changed her CV six times, has ten parking fines,
and still can't find any work.
But she will try and try, and can't understand why,
she's not looking to be Captain Kirk.

She needs money for rent, the money she had, she's spent,
and soon they'll evict her from her room.
She'll stack shelves, answer the phone, clean in your home,
anything at all, even vacuum and moon.

# Lancashire Larry

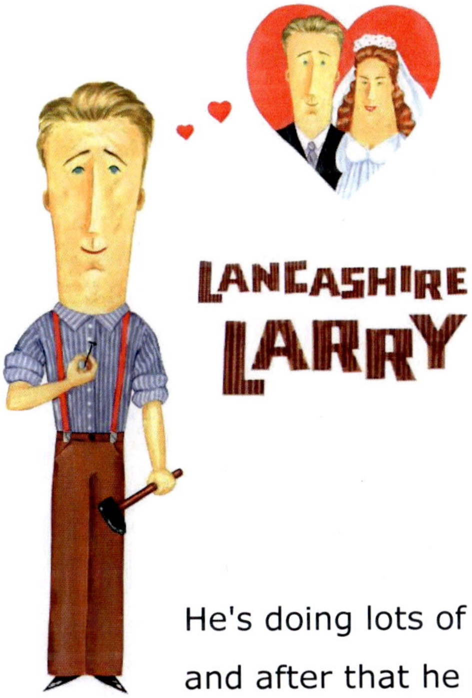


Lancashire Larry works in a cash and carry,
and saves all his money for his wedding.
He's decorating his place, and wants to replace,
all the carpets, curtains and bedding.

He's happy with his life, loves his future wife,
and is looking forward to their special day.
He can't pay for it all, especially the reception hall,
but luckily his parents have said they'd pay.

He's doing lots of overtime, working from nine to nine,
and after that he begins the decorating.
There's only twelve weeks to go, and it's going so slow,
but soon they'll both be celebrating.

## Lincolnshire Lynne

Lincolnshire Lynne reality likes to win,
and dreams of becoming a gymnast.
She plays twenty different sports,
has grade A reports and runs very fast.

She runs a three minute mile, does it in style,
and being in the Olympics is her dream.
Her coach is the best, she gets two days rest,
but she works really hard in between.

She's no fool, studies very hard at school,
and wants to take a degree in nutrition.
She's learning to sail, pays attention to detail,
and loves a really good competition.

## Beaufort Bob

Beaufort Bob used to steal and rob, but now he's trying to find work.
He's very strong, his life's gone wrong, and he's trying not to go berserk.

He used to work as a mechanic, but started to
panic, about the Police finding the stolen cars.
So he sold them to a mate, but it was a little late
and that's why he's spent time behind bars.

His life is now better, he rents a flat in Cheddar,
and his future is starting to look bright.
He's got a few mates, has been on two dates,
and is very determined to get it right!

# Cantal

Listen to Cantal and you'll be under her spell,
her singing is like that of a bird.
Everyone who's heard her sing, say the same thing,
it's the most beautiful voice they've heard.

When she sings people smile, they stand up in the aisle,
happy, clapping and humming.
Their worries disappear, they forget all about their fear,
and it feels like good fortune is coming.

She has sung for kings and queens, old people and teens,
and has even sung for the Pope.
She practices all day long, different ways to sing each song,
every note she sings, gives hope!

# Randolph Robiola

Randolph Robiola is a very fast bowler, with a family history of playing cricket.
But the team he is in, often lose, not win, so now it's his job to pick it.

They don't train, no one is to blame,
people just have other things to do.
They need a plan and Randolph is the man,
to organise this and follow it through.

They have the skills and techniques, haven't won in weeks,
and their motivation is very, very low.
To cheer them up, Randolph will show how to win the cup,
taking things very gently, nice and slow.

## Anetta Capretta

Anetta Capretta owns a pink Lambretta,
and at night sleeps with it by her bed.
It used to be green, but she wanted to be seen,
so decided to paint it pink instead.

A present from her dad, she was very, very glad,
that he didn't mind the pink paint.
She was a little afraid, after the money he'd paid,
he'd see it, scream and then faint!

But he said, ‘green, pink or red, and you keep it near your bed,
the colour pink causes me no worry.
It's the traffic on the roads, speeding trucks with heavy loads,
and the crazy people in such a hurry.'

## Kielbasa Kowalski

Kielbasa Kowalski often looses his house key, and once spent the night in his car.
He has Fiat 126, measuring two metres by six, it's not much bigger than his guitar.

There are beer cans on the floor, gherkins in the door,
and bread rolls that are three months old.
With cigarette ash on the dash, and two zloty in cash,
he's a quiet man, who looks dirty and old.

His Grandfather was Prussian, his father a Russian,
they hated anything coloured red.
His father's glad to be alive, pleased to survive,
all his other friends, they are dead.